SAMUEL MORSE, THAT'S WHO!

Tracy Nelson Maurer

illustrated by **el primo Ramón**

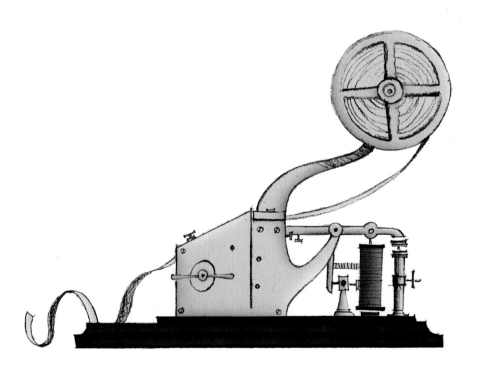

Henry Holt and Company • New York

Henry Holt and Company, *Publishers since 1866*

Henry Holt® is a registered trademark of Macmillan Publishing Group, LLC

175 Fifth Avenue, New York, NY 10010 • mackids.com

Library of Congress Cataloging-in-Publication Data

Names: Maurer, Tracy, 1965– author. | Primo Ramón, illustrator.

Title: Samuel Morse, that's who! : the story of the telegraph and Morse code / Tracy Nelson Maurer ;
    illustrated by El Primo Ramón.

Description: First edition, 2019. | New York : Henry Holt and Company, [2019] | Audience: Age 4–7.

Identifiers: LCCN 2018039225 | ISBN 9781627791304 (hardcover)

Subjects: LCSH: Morse, Samuel Finley Breese, 1791–1872—Juvenile literature. | Telegraph—History—
    Juvenile literature. | Morse code—Juvenile literature. | Inventors—United States—Biography—
    Juvenile literature. | Painters—United States—Biography—Juvenile literature.

Classification: LCC TK5243.M7 M37 2019 | DDC 621.383092 [B]—dc23

LC record available at https://lccn.loc.gov/2018039225

Our books may be purchased in bulk for promotional, educational, or business use. Please contact
your local bookseller or the Macmillan Corporate and Premium Sales Department at (800) 221-7945
ext. 5442 or by e-mail at MacmillanSpecialMarkets@macmillan.com.

First edition, 2019 / Designed by Liz Dresner

The art for this book was created as pencil line drawings, shadowed with soft pencil and charcoal,
and colored digitally.

Printed in China by RR Donnelley Asia Printing Solutions Ltd., Dongguan City, Guangdong Province

10 9 8 7 6 5 4 3 2 1

For -- . --. and - --- -- -- -.--, with love —T. N. M.

To Telmo, who will see a world we can't imagine —E. P. R.

Back when Samuel Morse was a boy, news wasn't usually *new* by the time folks heard it. A letter could ride for weeks between towns or sail for months between countries.

In the early 1800s, nothing traveled long distances fast. So, who would dream of instant messages?

Samuel Morse, that's who!

But first he dabbled with other inventions, though without much success.

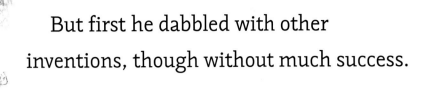

The water pump he designed with his brother? Almost nobody bought it.

His marble-cutting machine? Already patented.

He experimented with wild paint mixes, too—milk for a pearly effect, glazes for glossy finishes, even beer for some reason.

Truth be told, Samuel fancied himself an artist—and a fancy one at that. But he mostly painted portraits, tromping from town to town to earn money. His dream? Painting grand scenes—Hercules dying, Bible stories, historic battles. He believed his talent would raise America's *boorish* taste in art.

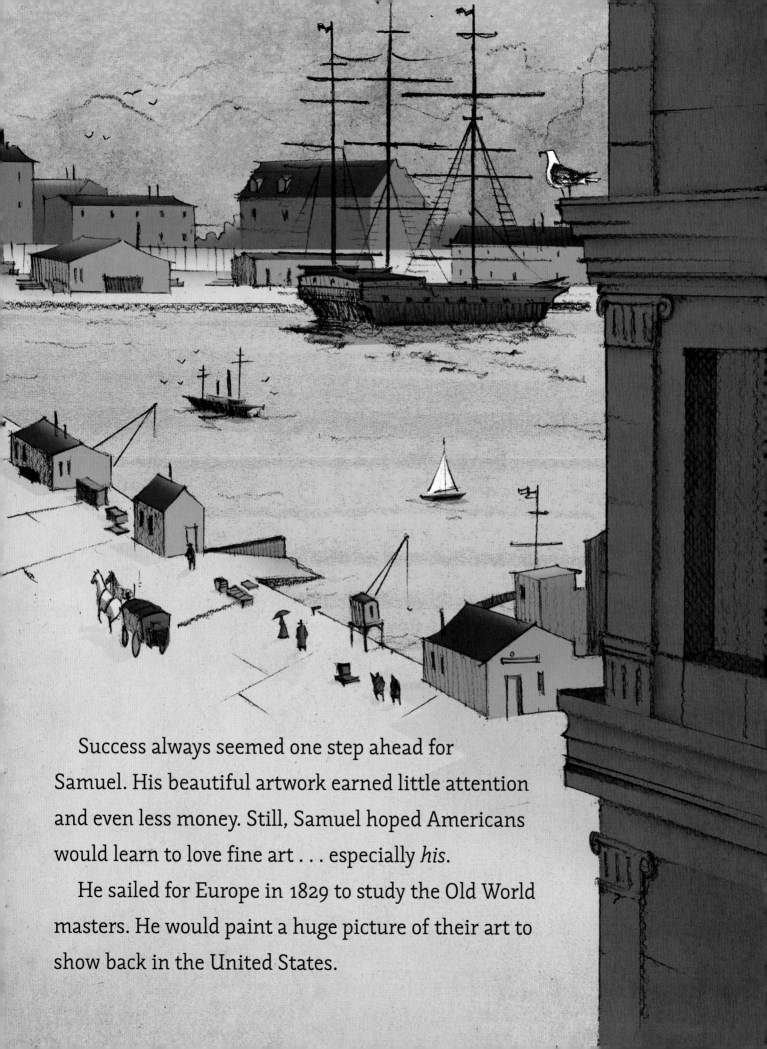

Success always seemed one step ahead for
Samuel. His beautiful artwork earned little attention
and even less money. Still, Samuel hoped Americans
would learn to love fine art . . . especially *his*.

He sailed for Europe in 1829 to study the Old World
masters. He would paint a huge picture of their art to
show back in the United States.

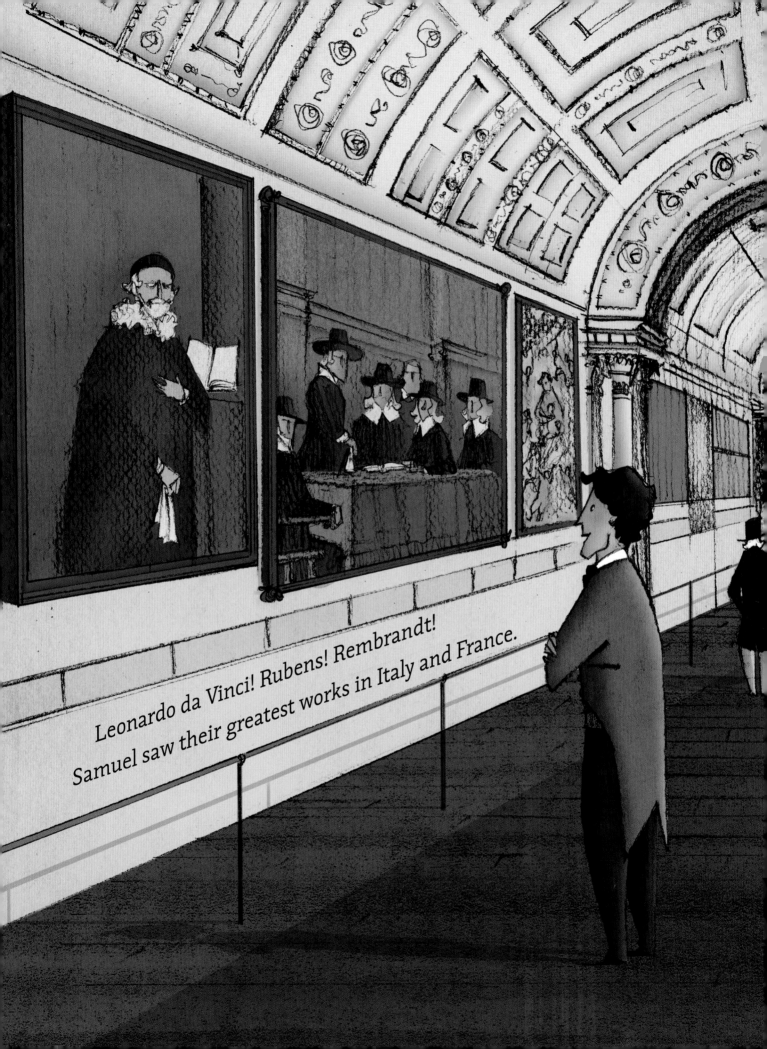

Leonardo da Vinci! Rubens! Rembrandt! Samuel saw their greatest works in Italy and France.

He also saw the famous French optical telegraph system in action. Created in 1794, it had served military leaders during wartime and had kept villages updated with news. Towers relayed nearly ten thousand possible codes for messages depending on the signal arm positions—if it wasn't foggy or dark.

Who could think of a better system?

Samuel Morse, that's who!

But not until he finished his masterpiece. Day after day for more than a year, he painted in France.

Samuel finally stored his massive painting aboard the good ship *Sully* and sailed for home in 1832.

Talk on deck drifted between not-so-new news and the possibilities for electricity. Was it simply a toy? Could this "liquid lightning" ever be useful? they wondered.

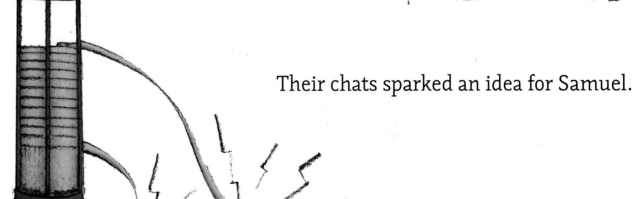

Their chats sparked an idea for Samuel.

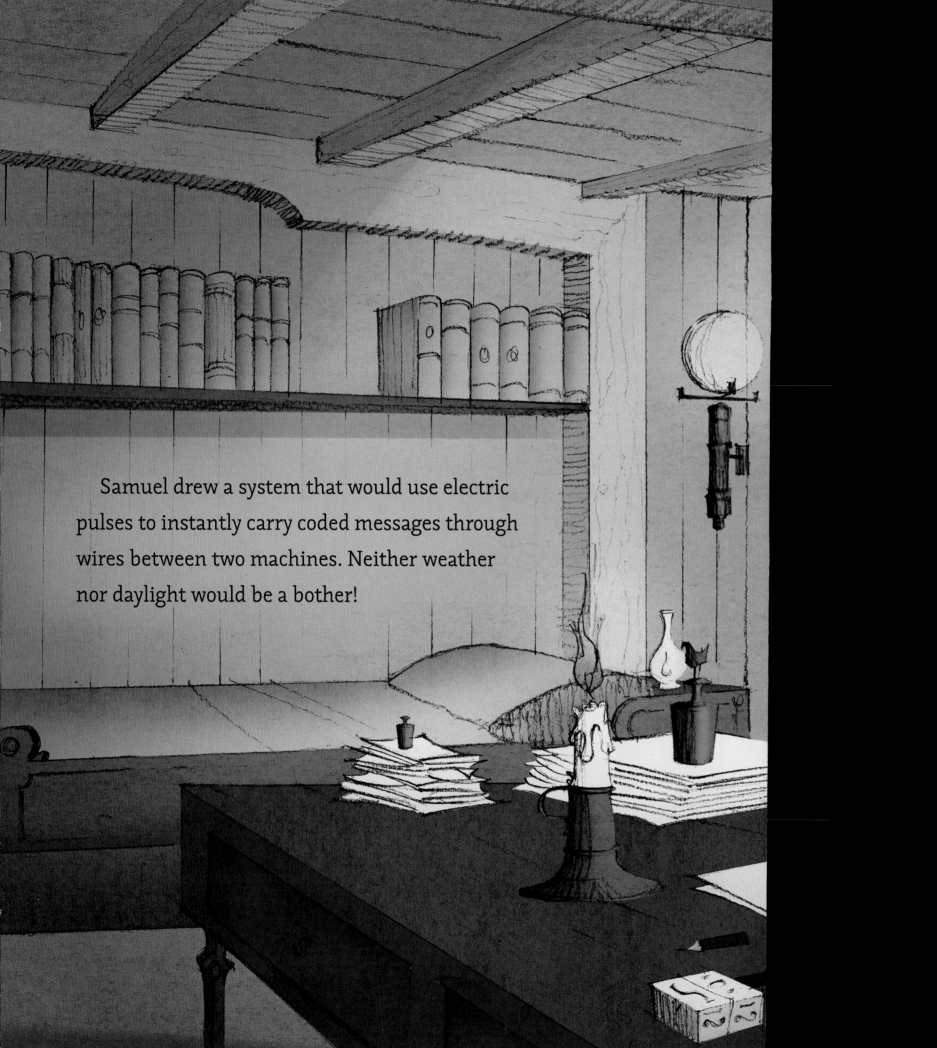

Samuel drew a system that would use electric pulses to instantly carry coded messages through wires between two machines. Neither weather nor daylight would be a bother!

Samuel also sketched a code using dots and dashes to stand for numbers. Each number meant a certain word. He figured he'd need about thirty thousand numbers—and one very big code book.

Back in New York City, Samuel proudly unveiled his masterpiece. And as before, not many people noticed.

Folks took great interest, however, in his ideas for an electromagnetic telegraph machine. Delightful! Amusing! But how would such an electric contraption ever be *useful*?

Who would show them?

Samuel Morse, that's who!

He began working in earnest on his telegraph. He experimented with an alphabet code. He gave the most frequently used letters the easiest symbols, to send messages faster. For example, just one dot could stand for an *E*.

Samuel also tinkered with clock parts to move a paper tape that recorded messages. He strung wires around his studio to test his work. But Samuel was still an artist at heart. He needed help.

He shared his idea with two friends, science professor Leonard Gale and the machine-minded Alfred Vail. The team clicked. Samuel set aside his paints to focus on the invention.

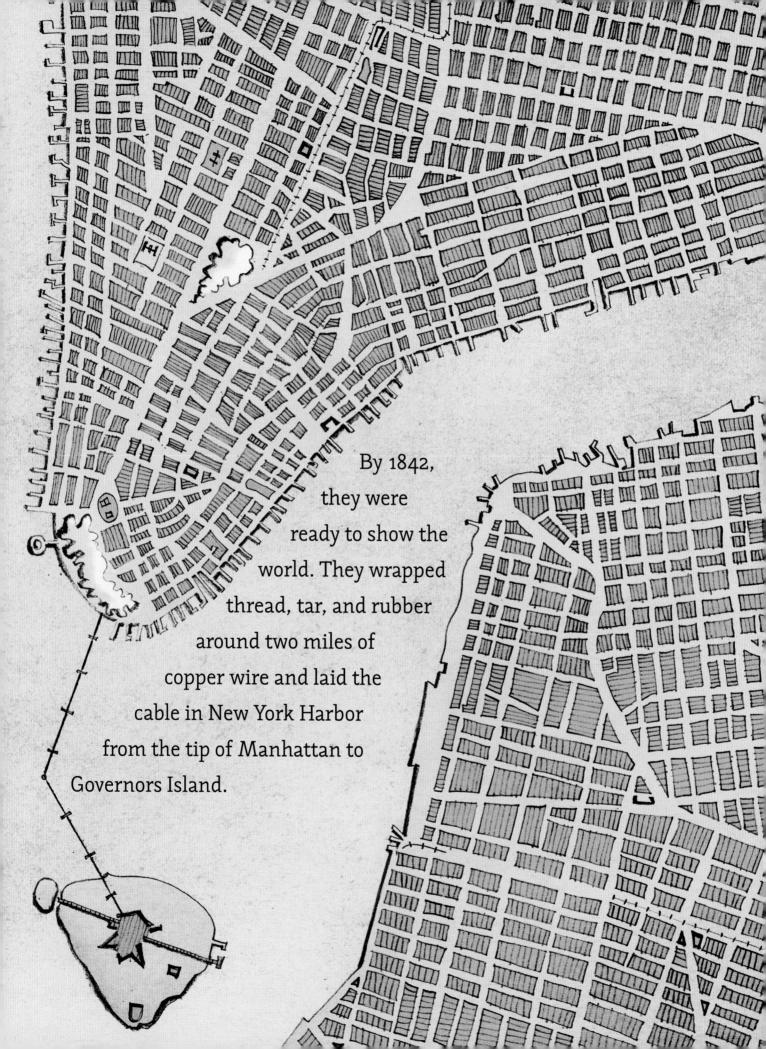

By 1842, they were ready to show the world. They wrapped thread, tar, and rubber around two miles of copper wire and laid the cable in New York Harbor from the tip of Manhattan to Governors Island.

A crowd gathered to watch.
Samuel began tapping the code
into his machine on one side of
the harbor.

Dit, ditty-dit, dit, dit!

In a blink, the machine on
the other side began to scratch
into the paper tape.

Dit, ditty-dit, dit, dit!

Amazing! People clapped and
cheered . . . until the line went dead.
Then they laughed at Samuel's crazy idea.

Samuel later learned that a ship
had pulled up his cable. Not knowing
what the wire was, the crew had cut
it and thrown it back into the water.

Samuel asked the US Congress to fund a telegraph line between Baltimore and Washington, DC. After a long and blustery debate, Congress agreed. Samuel set his deadline for December 1843.

Delay followed delay. Samuel's team finally set to digging trenches along the route in October. They buried the cable in lead pipes. Then, with only months left—*crash!* The trenching plow hit a boulder and crumpled.

While it was repaired, Samuel
tested their work so far . . .

Nothing!
The team discovered that poorly made pipes had
caused the wires to fail in damp soil. Samuel needed
another plan—and fast.

It stood to reason that if the wire didn't work *below* ground, then perhaps the best solution was *above* ground.

In March, the team went back to work. They strung wires between tall chestnut poles. They covered about a mile a day, rain or shine.

The telegraph line crossed into Baltimore more than a week ahead of the demonstration planned for May 24, 1844.

The big day came. Samuel sat at his machine in the US Supreme Court chamber. His assistant, Alfred Vail, set up his machine in a Baltimore train depot.

Samuel tapped a coded message to Alfred.

Then he waited.

Moments later, the machine clattered.

Dit-dah-dah! Dit-dit-dit-dit!

Alfred had replied with the same message:

WHAT HATH GOD WROUGHT

.-- .... .- - / .... .- - .... / --. --- -.. / .-- .-. --- ..- --. .... -

Success!

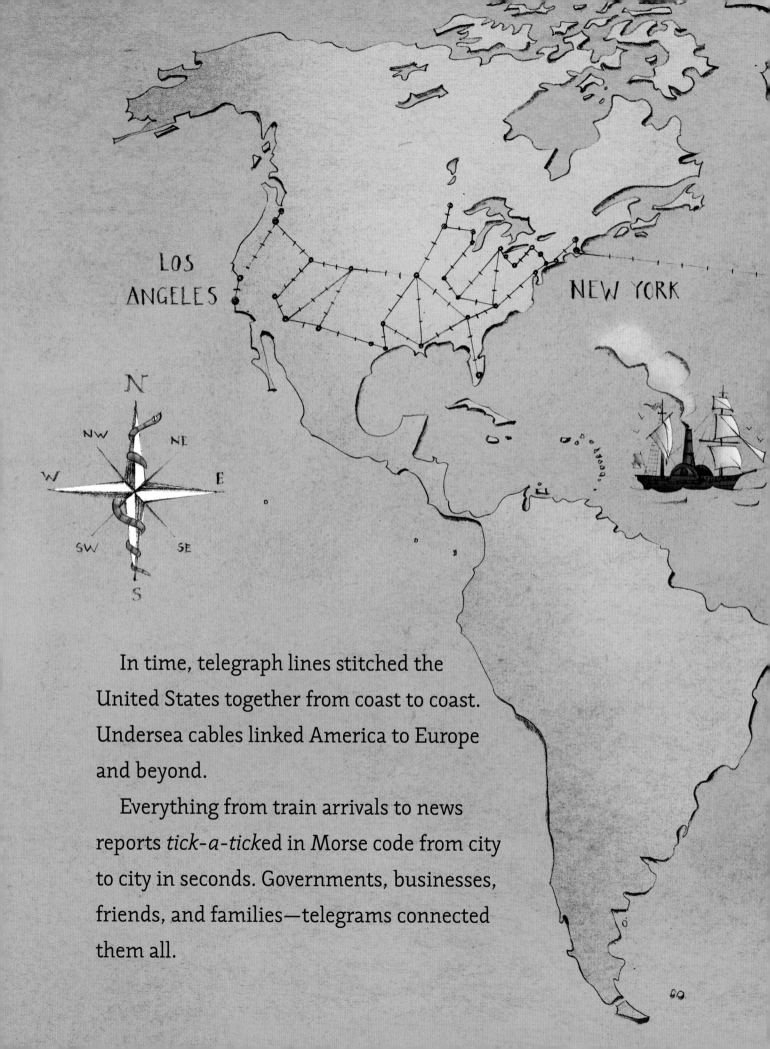

LOS ANGELES

NEW YORK

N
NW   NE
W   E
SW   SE
S

In time, telegraph lines stitched the United States together from coast to coast. Undersea cables linked America to Europe and beyond.

Everything from train arrivals to news reports *tick-a-tick*ed in Morse code from city to city in seconds. Governments, businesses, friends, and families—telegrams connected them all.

BERLIN

PARIS

THE
ORES

So, who made
electricity useful?
Who created instant
messages and changed
the world forever?

...amuel M---r...e, that's who!

Samuel Finley Breese Morse

April 27, 1791–April 2, 1872

Time Line

1791—Samuel Finley Breese Morse is born in Charlestown, Massachusetts

1805—Enters Yale College; graduates in 1810

1811—Studies at London's Royal Academy of Arts, led by American Benjamin West

1815—Returns to the United States in October after the War of 1812 ends

1818—Marries Lucretia Pickering Walker; they later have three children

1825—Receives a fee of about $1,000 to paint the Revolutionary War hero Marquis de Lafayette

1825—Lucretia dies in Connecticut; she's buried before Morse receives the news in Washington

1826—Starts the National Academy of Design in New York and begins art lectures

1827—Helps found the *New York Journal of Commerce*

1829—Sails for Europe; he later becomes friends with James Fenimore Cooper in Rome

1832—Returns to America aboard the *Sully*, jotting his ideas for an electric telegraph system in his sketchbook on the journey

1833—Displays his masterpiece, *Gallery of the Louvre*, in New York

1834—Sells *Gallery of the Louvre* for a disappointing $1,200

1838—Demonstrates his telegraph to President Martin Van Buren

1839—Meets Louis Daguerre in France, which sparks his interest in photography

1840—Receives a US patent for his telegraph

1843—Congress sets aside $30,000 to build and test a telegraph line

1844—Sends first long-distance telegraph message; a line opens for business

1848—Marries Sarah Elizabeth Griswold

1858—First successful transatlantic telegraph cable is installed

1861—Civil War begins; both sides use the telegraph to communicate

1861—First transcontinental telegraph line replaces the Pony Express for delivering news to the West

1872—Dies in New York, four years before Alexander Graham Bell patents the telephone

1982—*Gallery of the Louvre* sells for $3.25 million, then a record for a work by an American painter

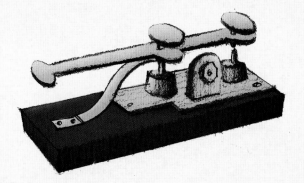

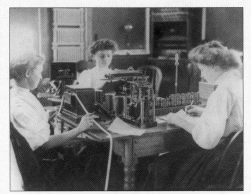

Women telegraph operators, 1908

Telegraphy, the high-tech communication of its time, created one of the few paying jobs open outside the home to women (although typically only white women). They worked as telegraph operators, sending and receiving telegrams, often for less money than men would be paid. Some of the earliest trade schools for women in America and Europe taught telegraphy skills.

Tap Into More Facts About
Samuel Morse and Telegraph History

- Samuel Morse helped introduce Louis Daguerre's camera technology in America. For a while, Morse took photographic portraits instead of painting them. He helped train America's first photographers, including Mathew Brady, whose Civil War images became famous.

- By the 1850s, telegraph operators were *listening* to the code rather than reading printed tapes. Dots were *dits*. Dashes were *dahs*. It was like music!

- During the Civil War, telegraphists were at risk of capture by the opposing side. Enemy soldiers would force operators to intercept military messages or send fake information to the opposing army.

- The last Western Union telegram was sent in 2006. Western Union was the best-known US telegraph company; it continues to provide financial services.

- Some Boy Scouts, amateur radio operators, pilots, sailors, and soldiers still learn Morse code.

- January 11 is Learn Your Name in Morse Code Day. Use the translator at morsecode.scphillips.com /translator.html.

SOS is recognized worldwide as the call for help.

In Morse code, it looks like this:

... --- ...

Samuel Morse's original American Morse Code was updated in 1851 to the International Morse Code, which is what people around the world still use today. Images and text in this book are also based on International Morse Code.

Bibliography

Many articles, books, and websites offer information about Samuel Morse. Most focus on his telegraph, but others illuminate his artistic life as well. Here are a few that were particularly helpful to me.

Print

Alter, Judy. *Samuel F. B. Morse: Inventor and Code Creator*. Chanhassen, MN: Child's World, 2003.

Brownlee, Peter John, ed. *Samuel F. B. Morse's "Gallery of the Louvre" and the Art of Invention*. New Haven, CT: Yale University Press, 2014.

Kurin, Richard. *The Smithsonian's History of America in 101 Objects*. New York: Penguin, 2013.

Mabee, Carleton. *The American Leonardo: A Life of Samuel F. B. Morse*. Fleischmanns, NY: Purple Mountain Press, 2000.

McCormick, Anita. *The Invention of the Telegraph and Telephone in American History*. Berkeley Heights, NJ: Enslow, 2004.

Morse, Samuel F. B. *Samuel F. B. Morse: His Letters and Journals in Two Volumes*, Vol. 1, edited by Edward Lind Morse. Boston: Houghton Mifflin, 1914. Softcover reprint, Lexington, KY: Filiquarian, 2013.

Silverman, Kenneth. *Lightning Man: The Accursed Life of Samuel F. B. Morse*. Cambridge, MA: Da Capo Press, 2004.

Online

A&E Television Networks. "Samuel F. B. Morse." Biography.com. Updated Jan. 6, 2016. biography.com/people/samuel-morse.

Jepsen, Thomas. "Research Resources for the History of Telegraphy and the Work of Women in the Telegraph Industry." The Telegrapher Web Page. Society for the History of Technology. Updated Nov. 4, 2017. mindspring.com/~tjepsen/Teleg.html.

Library of Congress. "Artist, Politician, Photographer." Samuel F. B. Morse Papers, 1793 to 1919. loc.gov/collection/samuel-morse-papers/articles-and-essays/artist-politician-photographer/#artist-politician-photographer.

Author's Note

During an earlier research project, I noticed Morse's signature on a prominent portrait of Noah Webster. Was this the same Samuel F. B. Morse who developed the telegraph and created Morse code? How was a world-famous inventor also a painter? I had to know more! Over time, I came to appreciate artist Samuel F. B. Morse's story of creativity and ingenuity. He visualized words in a new binary language (computers today also use a binary language). He imagined using electricity as no one had done before. Then he made it all happen! He led his team through tests and revisions, again and again, until they proved the system worked. I admire his tenacity, his passion, and, above all, his creativity as an inventor and artist. I hope readers are inspired as well.

Notably, Morse did not work alone; I am also deeply grateful to many brilliant and gracious people: Christian Trimmer, Jessica Anderson, Jennifer Healey, and the team at Henry Holt; the talented Borja Ramón López Cotelo (el primo Ramón); Kenneth Snodgrass at Samuel Morse's Locust Grove Estate; Charlotte Todd and everyone at the Telegraph Museum Porthcurno, England; Kendra Marcus at BookStop Literary Agency; copyeditor Sherri Schmidt; writers and readers Sally Doherty, Thomas Jepsen, Ann Matzke, Joyce Sidman, Michelle Lackner, Tunie Munson-Benson, Laura Purdie Salas, Mary Bevis, Julie Lundgren, Shannon Peterson, and Melissa Martyr-Wagner; and my supportive family: Mike, Meg, and Tommy. Any mistakes or omissions are mine alone.

—T. N. M.

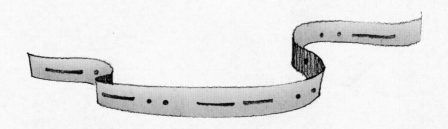